Italian states before the beginning of the Italian Wars in 1494.

I took these photos at the 2010 Carnevale in Venice in early February 2010.

Masks at the Carnival of Venice, with the "Bauta" mask shown on the left.

A Medico della Peste mask.

Arlecchino's half-mask is painted black with an ape-like nose and a "bump" to signify a devil's horn

A leather version of a Zanni mask, profile view

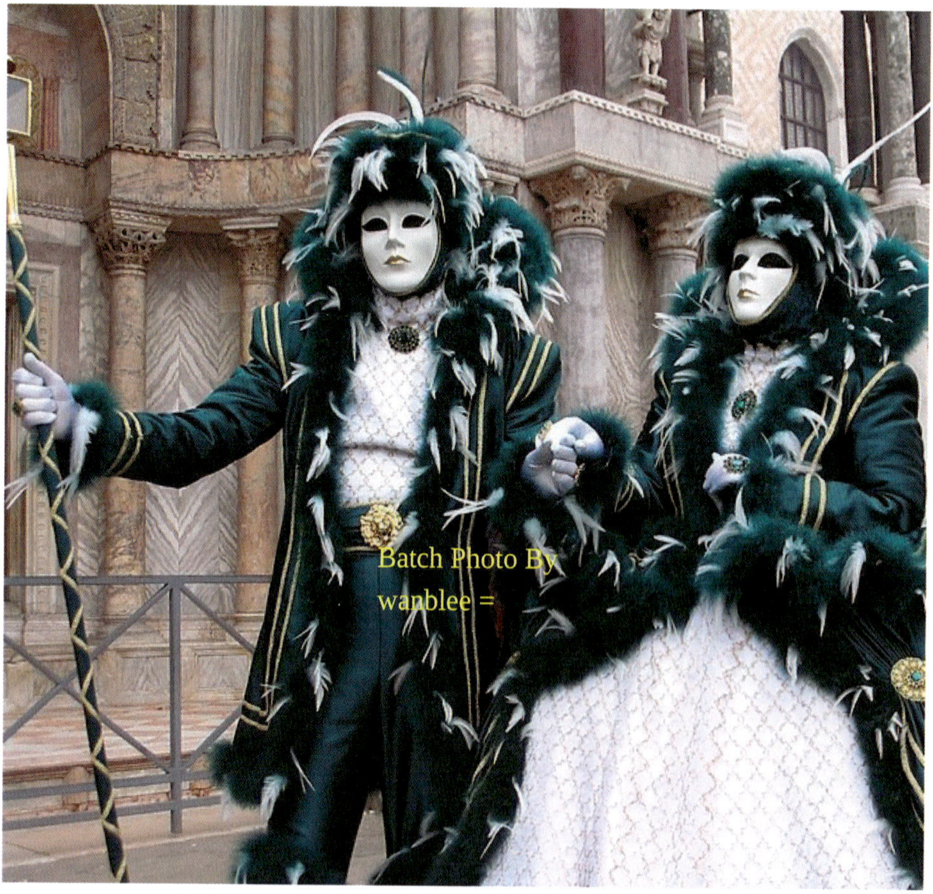
Batch Photo By
wanblee =

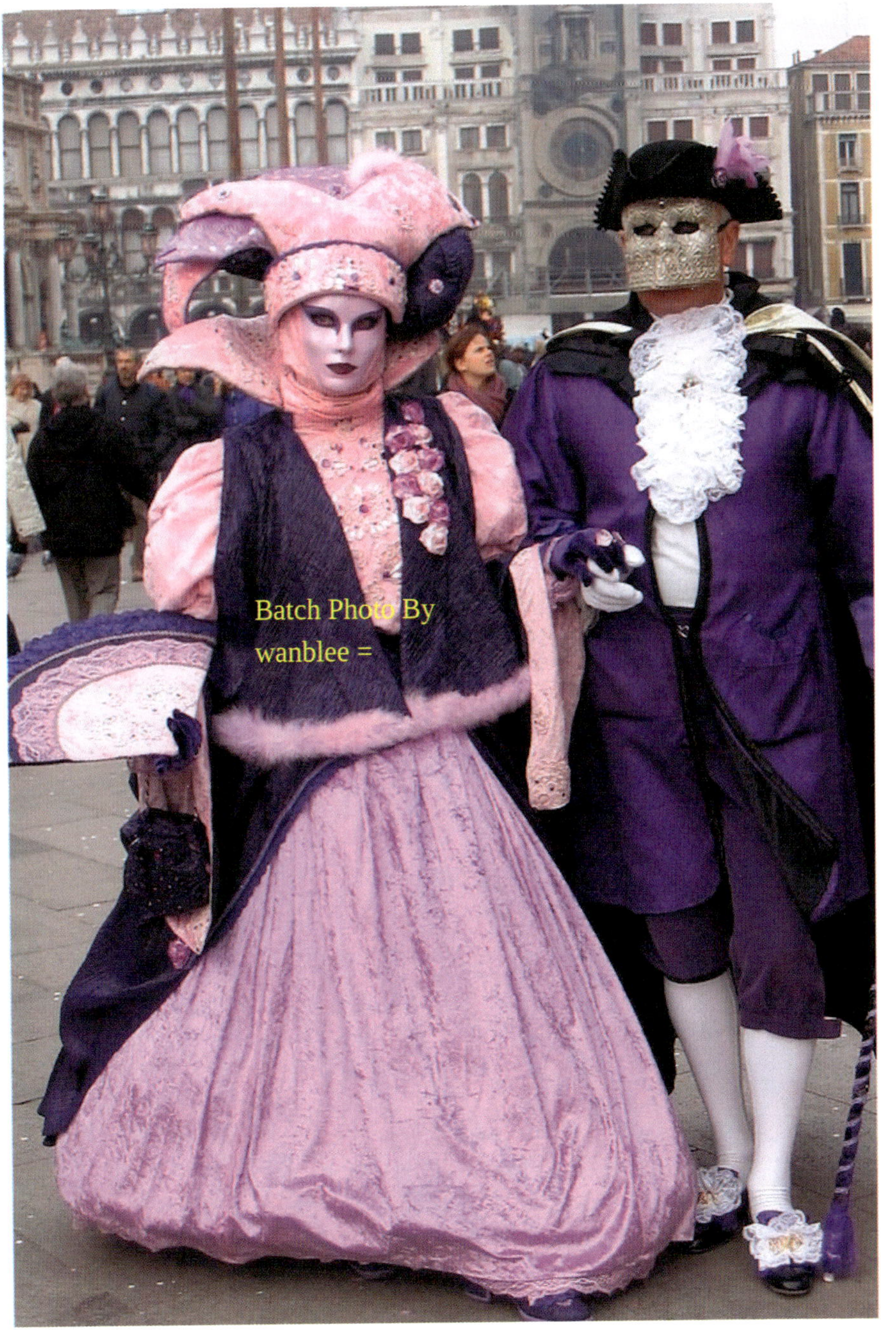
Batch Photo By
wanblee =

Carnival of Venice, Feb. 2007.

Carnival of Venice, Feb. 2007.

Carnevale di Venezia, 2007

Maschere al Carnevale di Venezia
2008

Carnival of Venice.

Carnevale di Venezia

Carnival of Venice.

Carnival of Venice.

Batch Photo By wanblee =

Mask Cat Carnival
Venice Artifact
Artwork Art

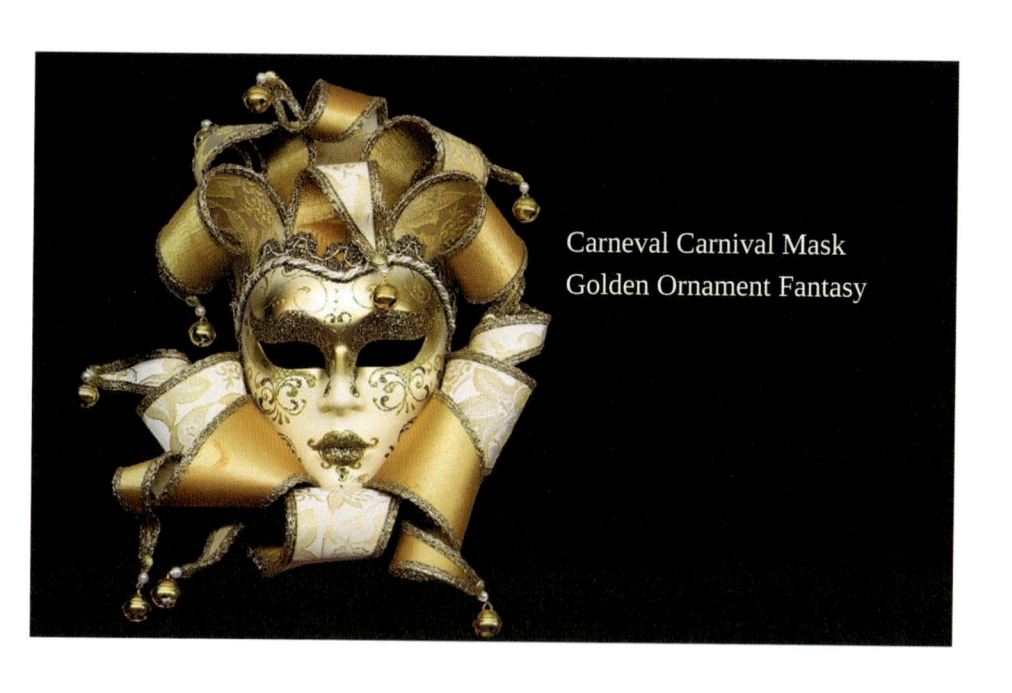

Carneval Carnival Mask
Golden Ornament Fantasy

Carnival Venice Eyes
Mask Woman

Carneval Carnival
Mask Golden Ornament
Fantasy

Mask Carneval
Carnival Mysterious
Ornament

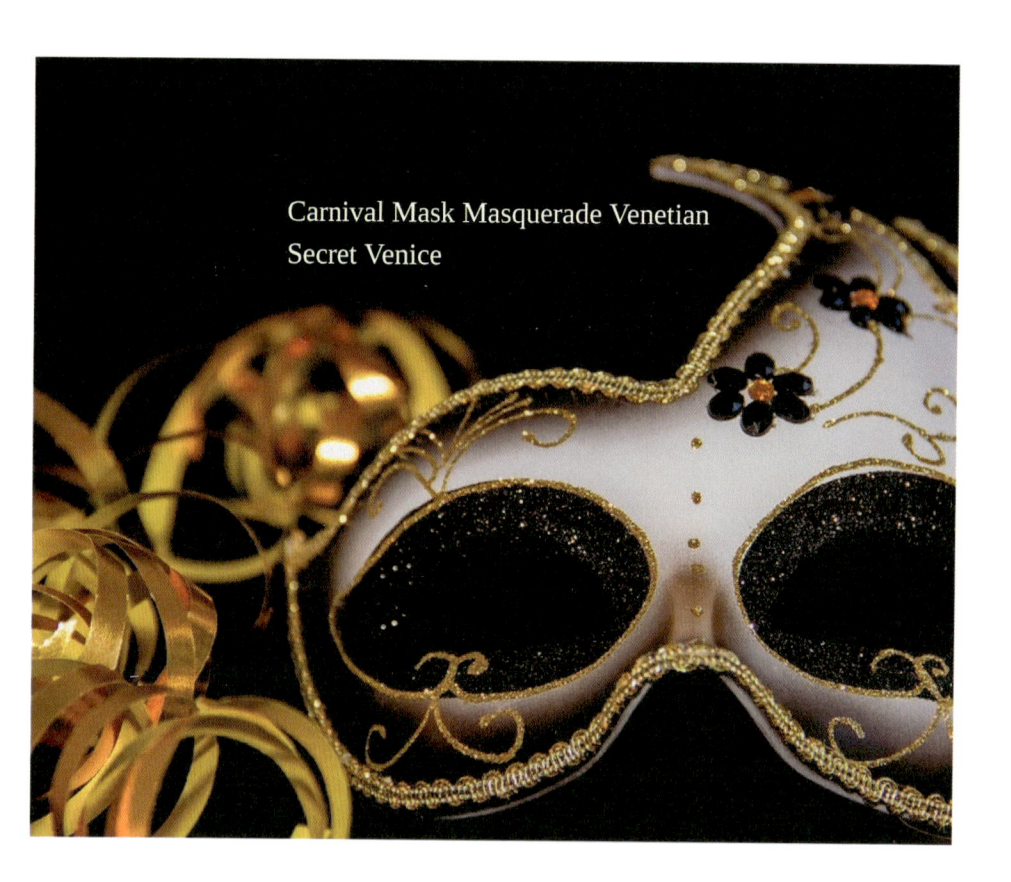

Carnival Mask Masquerade Venetian Secret Venice

Carnival Mask Celebration
Venetian Masquerade

Carnival Mask Venice Disguise Costume

Venice Mask People Costume Bauta Hat Carnival

Mask Carnival Venice
Mysterious Close Romance

Mask Carnival Venice

Costume Mystery Masked Ball Hide Traditional

Masks Mask Of Venice Carnival Venice Venice

Mask Carnival Venice
Mysterious Close Romance

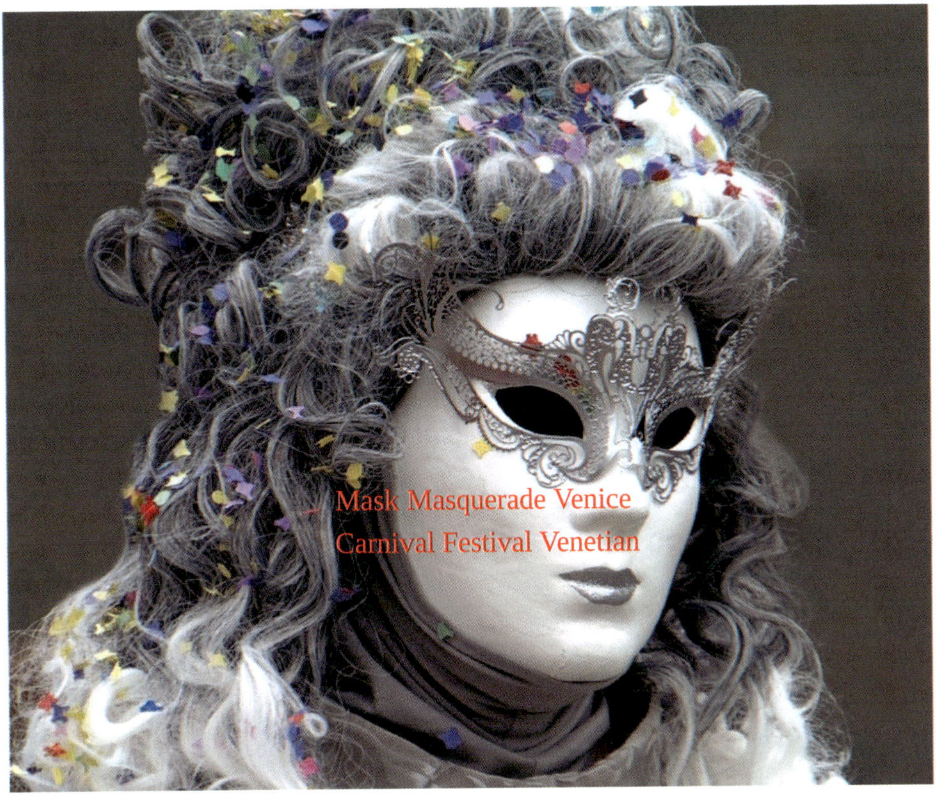
Mask Masquerade Venice
Carnival Festival Venetian

Carnival Mask Black Fun Masquerade Venice Colors

Venice Carnevale Costume
Carnival Venetian

Mask Carnival Venice Art Abstract Watercolor

Venice Italy Mask Venezia Carnival Costume

Mask Carnival Venice Mysterious Close Romance

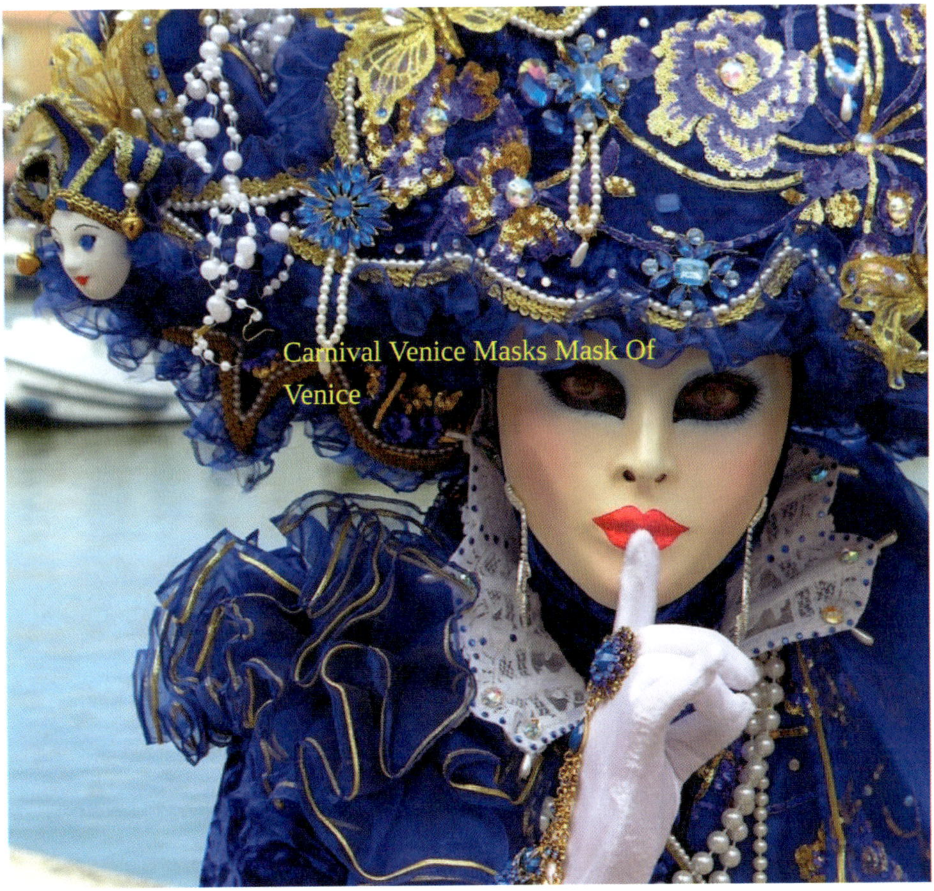
Carnival Venice Masks Mask Of
Venice

Mask Carnival Venice

Mask Of Venice Venice
Carnival Venice Blue Girl

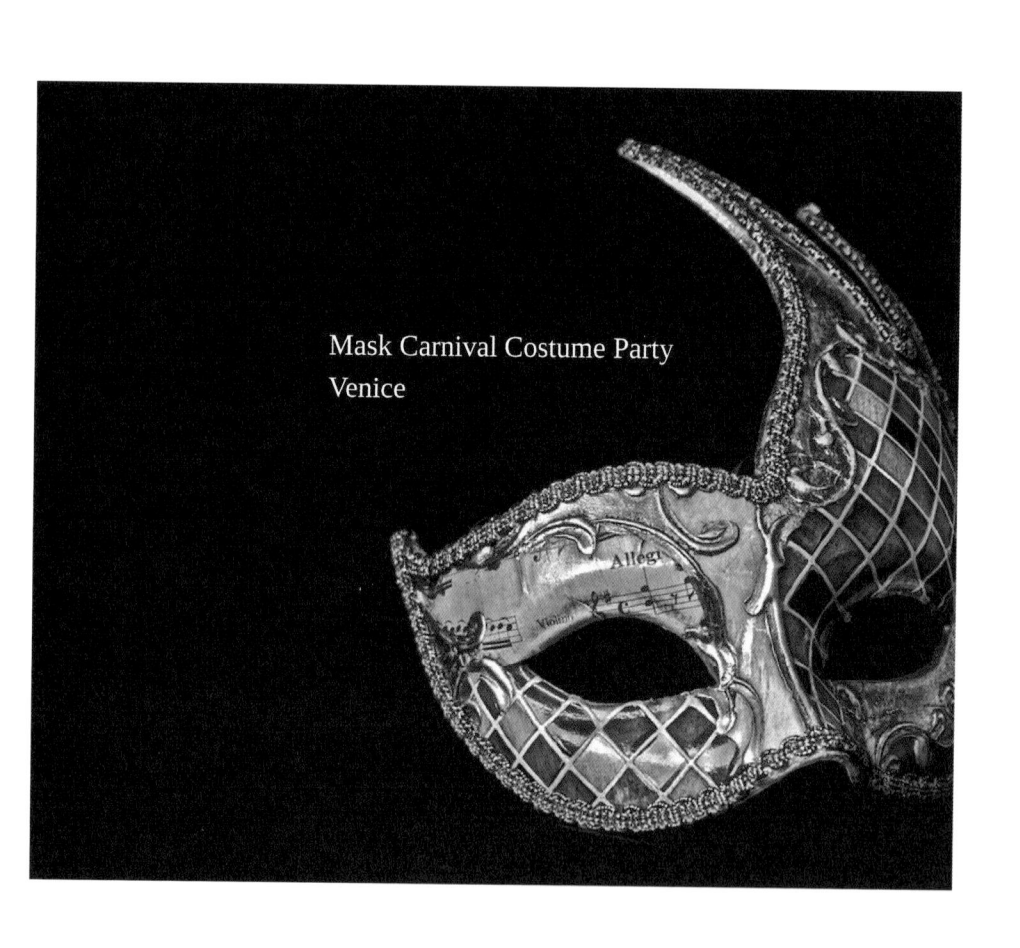

Mask Carnival Costume Party
Venice

Italy Venice Europe Masks Carnival

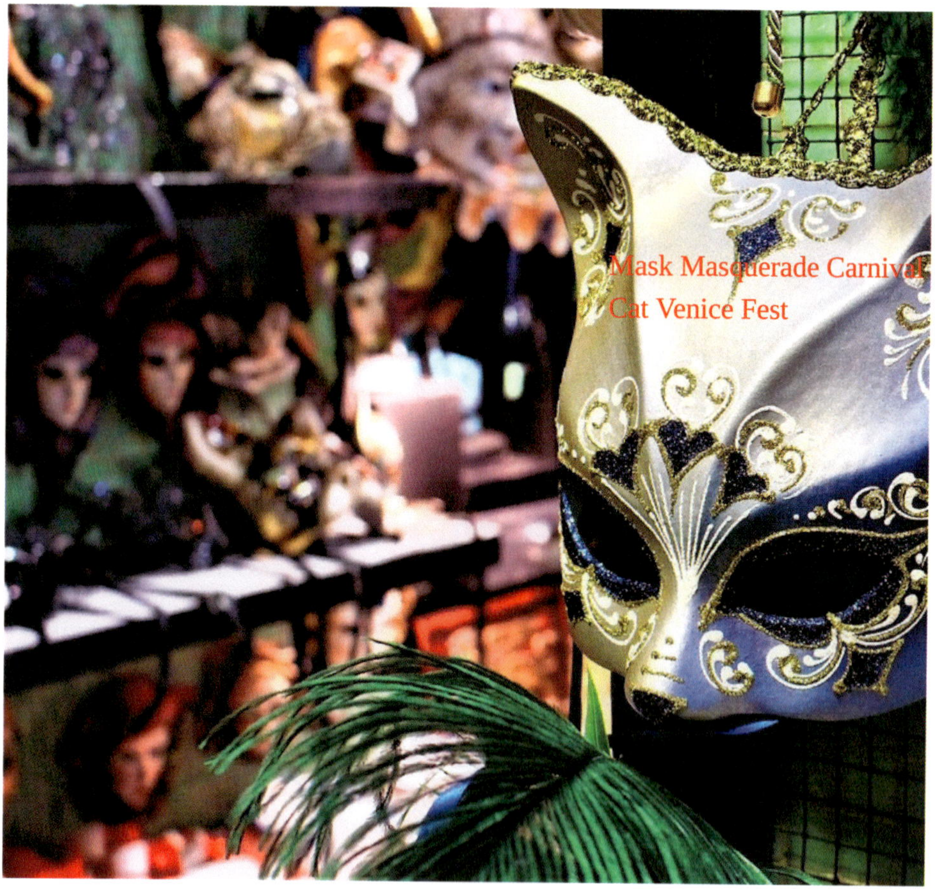
Mask Masquerade Carnival
Cat Venice Fest

Mask Mask Of Venice Carnival Venice

Mask Carnival Venice
Mysterious Close Romance

Venice Carnival Mask Party Masquerade Festival

Masks Gold Venice Carnival Face

Mask Venice Carnival Venice

Venice Italy Carnival

Mask Mask Of Venice Carnival Venice

Venice Mask Mask Of Venice Carnival Of Venice

Mask Of Venice Carnival Of Venice Masks Disguise

Mask Of Venice
Masks

Venice Venice Carnival Mask Costume Panel Carnival

Carnival Of Venice Mask Of
Venice Masks Disguise

Mask Carnival Confetti Streamer Colorful Venice

Venice Mask Red Carnival Italy Carnival Of Venice

Carnival Venice Mask Italy Costume Panel

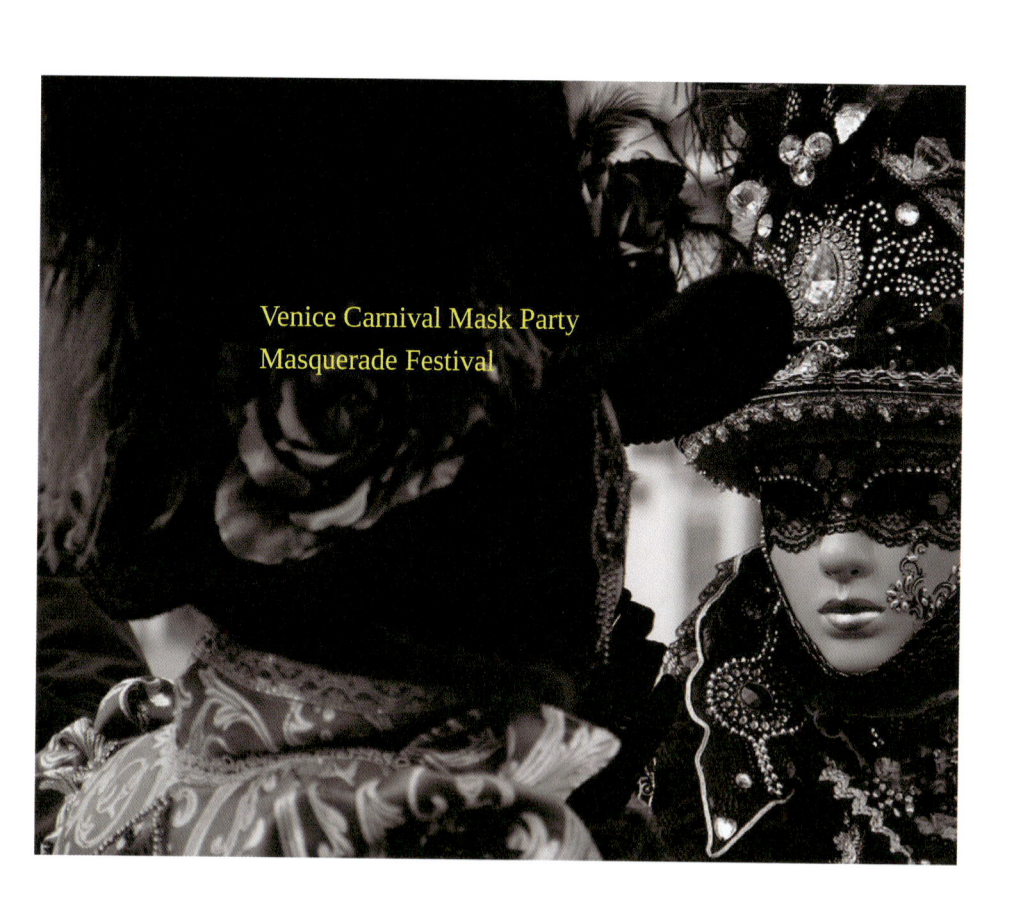

Venice Carnival Mask Party
Masquerade Festival

Mask Carnival Venice

Mask Pulcinella Pulcinella Mask Nose Theater

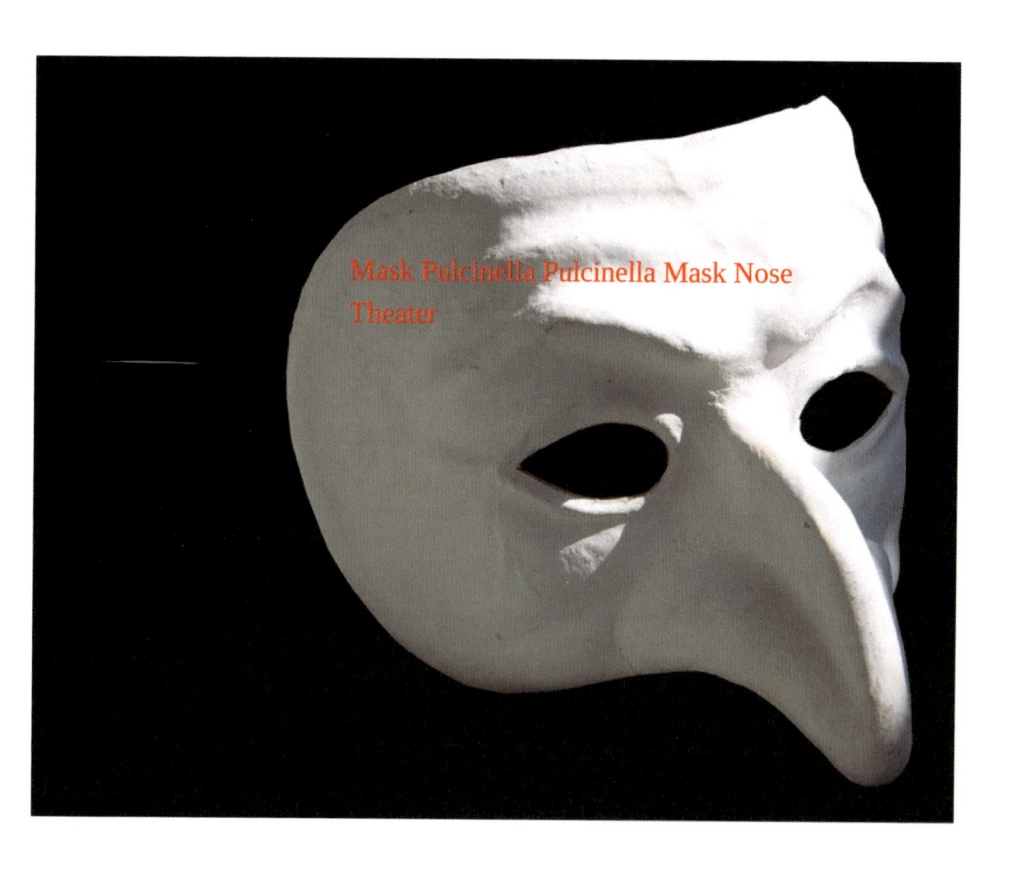

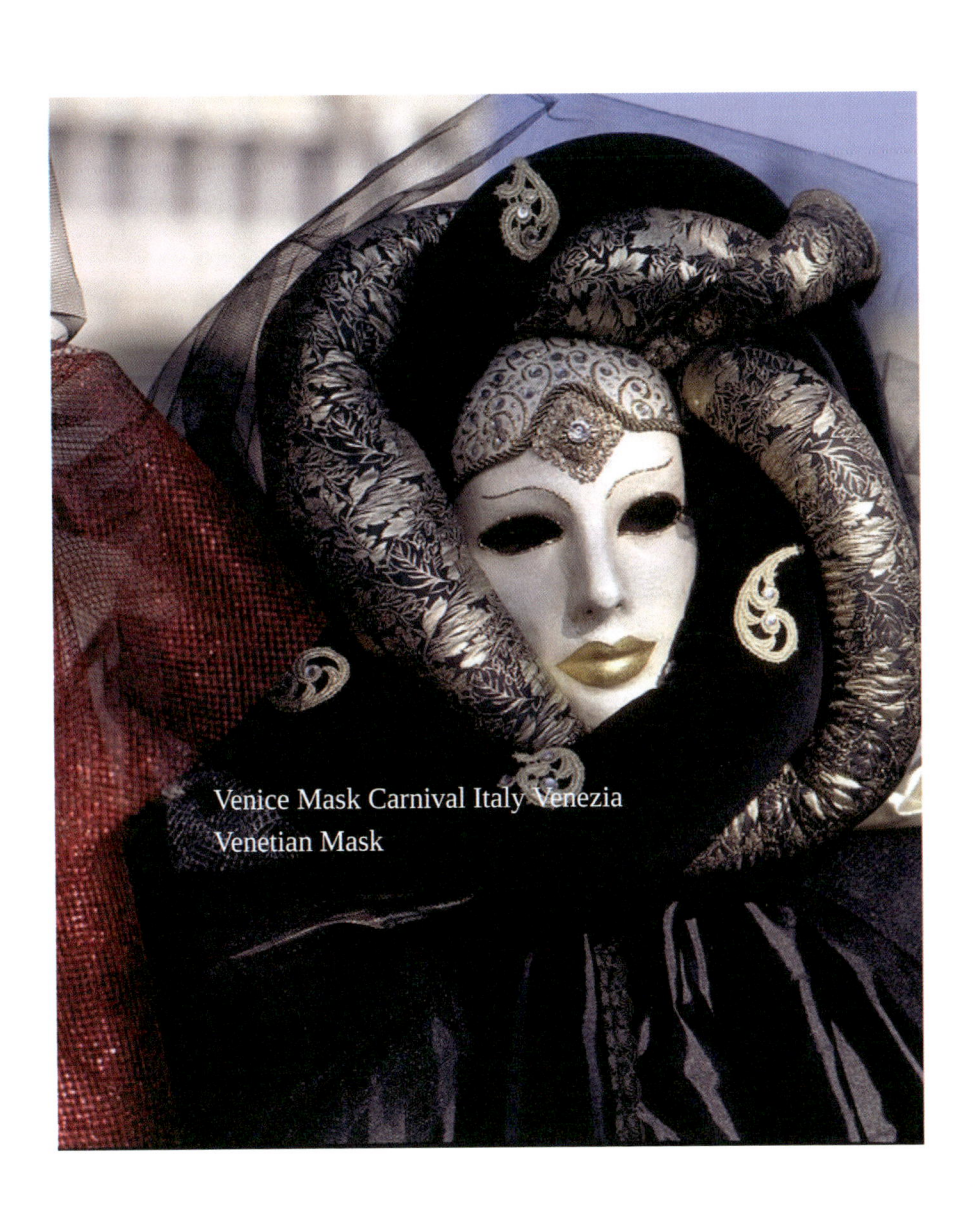

Venice Mask Carnival Italy Venezia
Venetian Mask

Venice Italy Carnival

Mask Of Venice Carnival Of Venice Masks

Venice Italy Mask Carnival Masks Of Venice

Venice Carnival Costume

Masks Of Venice
Masks Carnival Of Venice

Masks Carnival Of Venice Masks Of Venice

Mask Carnival Confetti Colorful Venice Mysterious

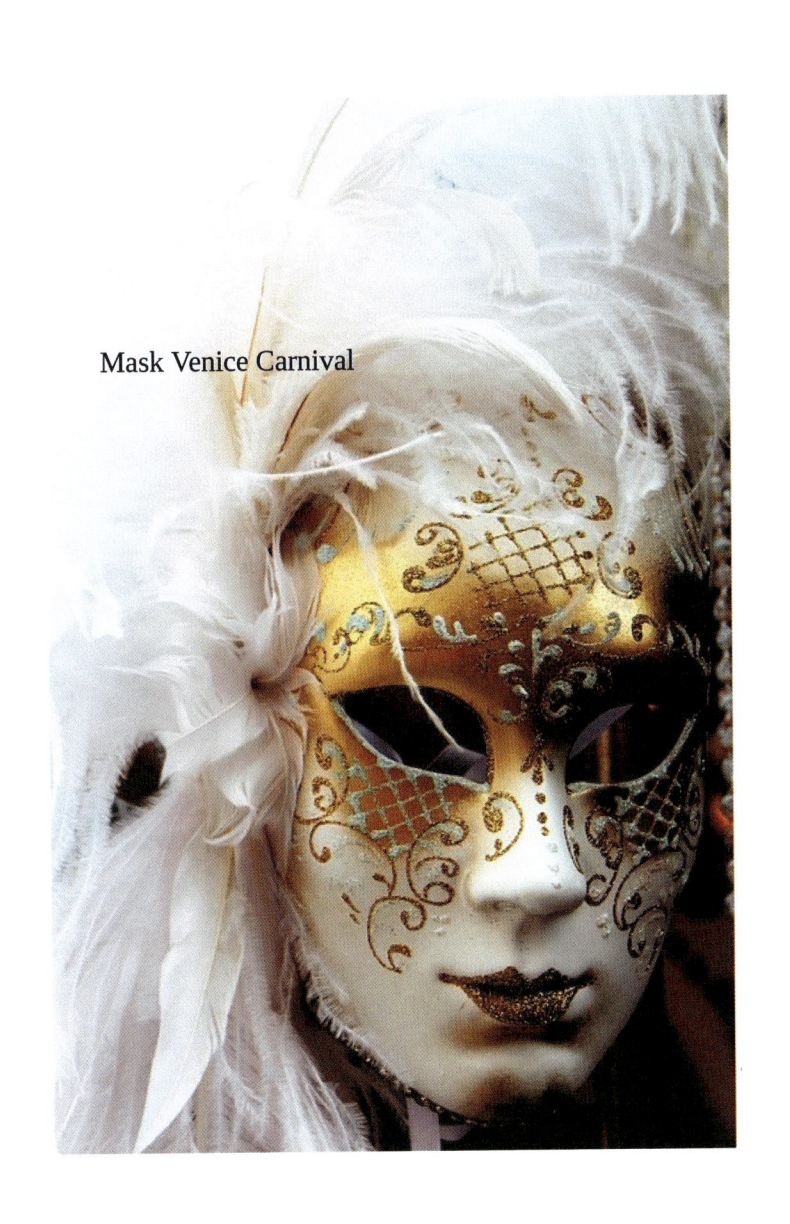

Mask Venice Carnival

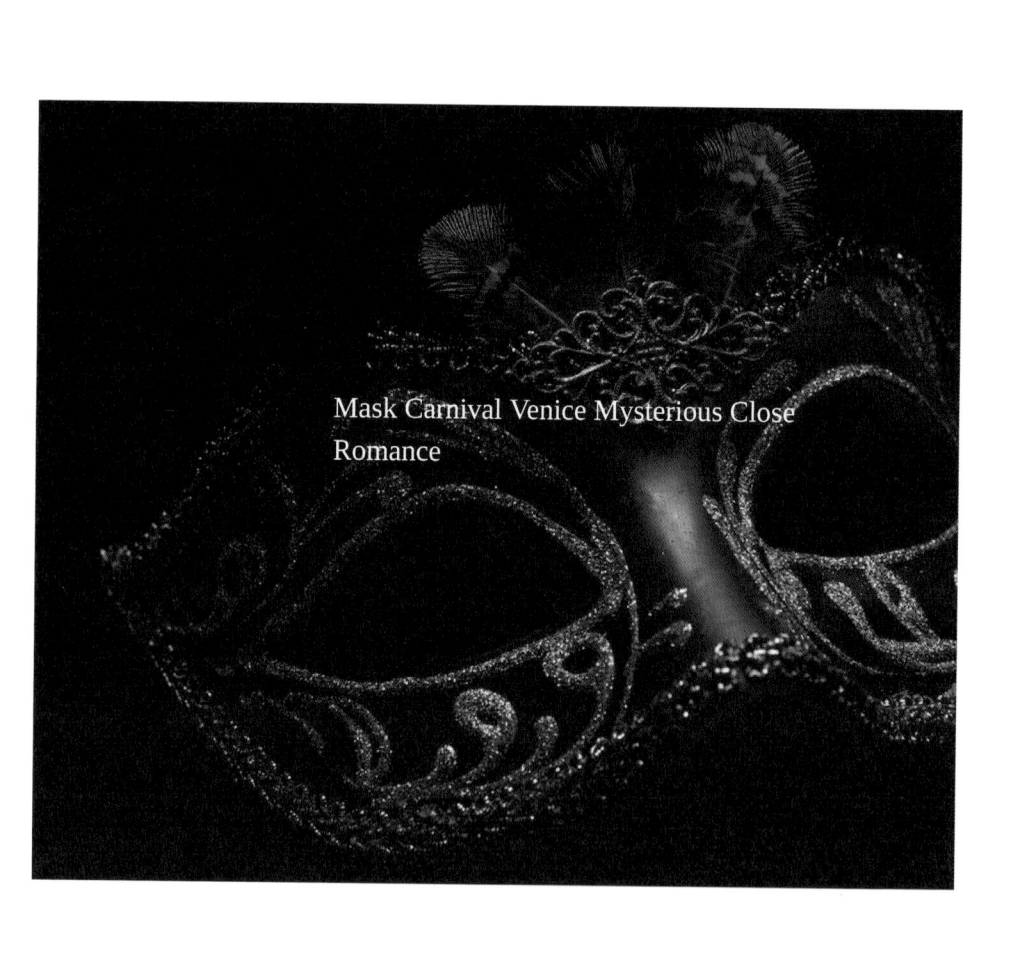

Mask Carnival Venice Mysterious Close Romance

Masks Disguise Venice Masquerade Carnival Party

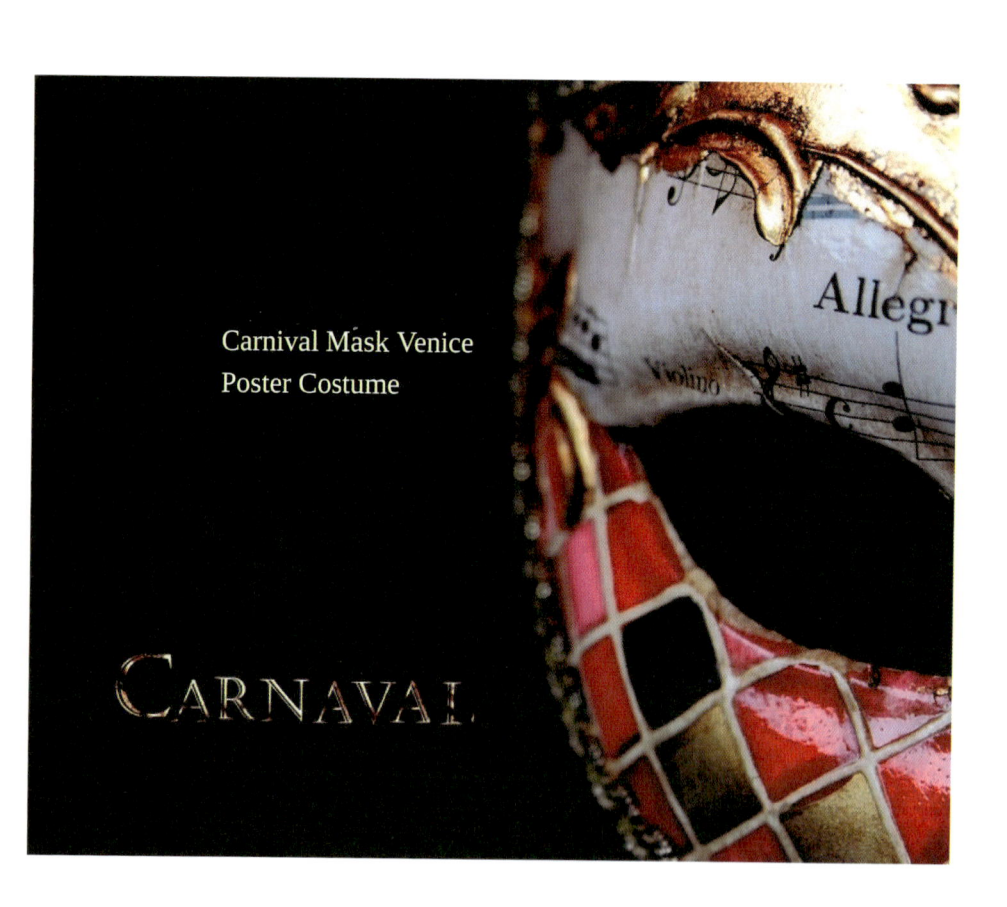

Carnival Mask Venice
Poster Costume

CARNAVAL

Venice
Costume Mask
Carnevale
Carnival
Venetian

The Carnival Of
Venice Mask
Italy

Mask Carnival Venice
Anonymous Colors Costume

Carnival Panel Mask Venice Make Up Fool-Time

Mask Of Venice Carnival Of Venice Venice Masks

Venice Mask Italy
Venezia Carnival
Venetian Mask

Mask Carnival Venice Mysterious Close Romance

Masks Carnival Venice Italy
Masquerade

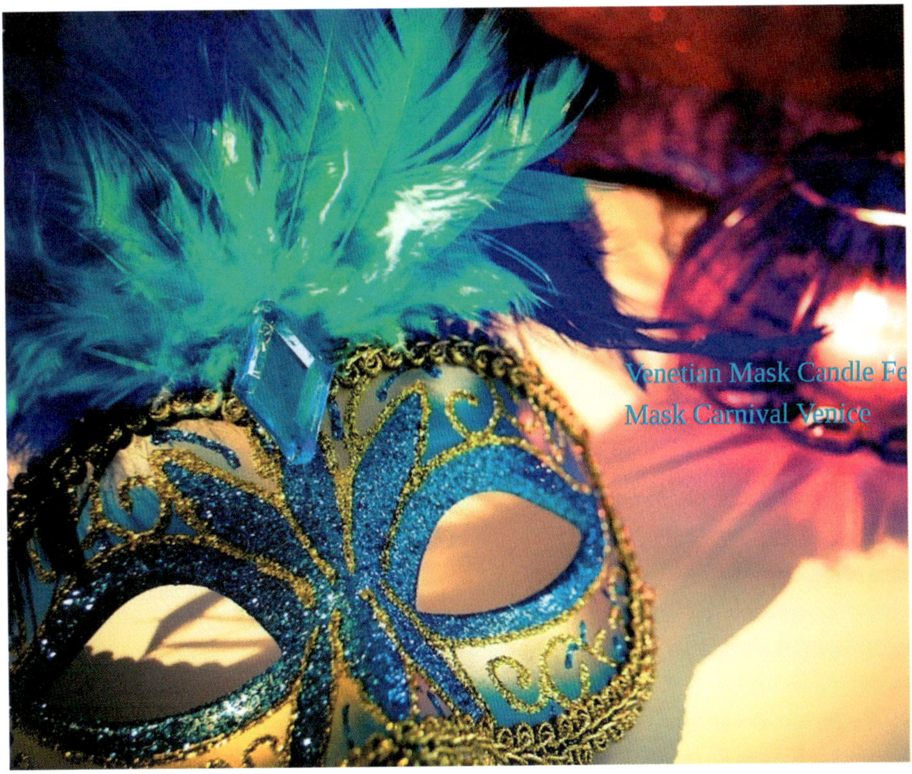
Venetian Mask Candle Fe
Mask Carnival Venice

Carnival Of Venice Mask Of Venice Masks

The Carnival Of Venice Mask Italy

Mask Venice Costume Carnival Disguise

Mask Carnival Confetti Streamer Colorful Venice

Masks Venice Carnival
Venice

Venice Italy Carnival

Venice Mask Of Venice Carnival Of Venice

Mask Pulcinella
Pulcinella Mask Nose
Theater

Mask Carnival Venice Mysterious Close Romance

Carnival Venice Ma
Carneval

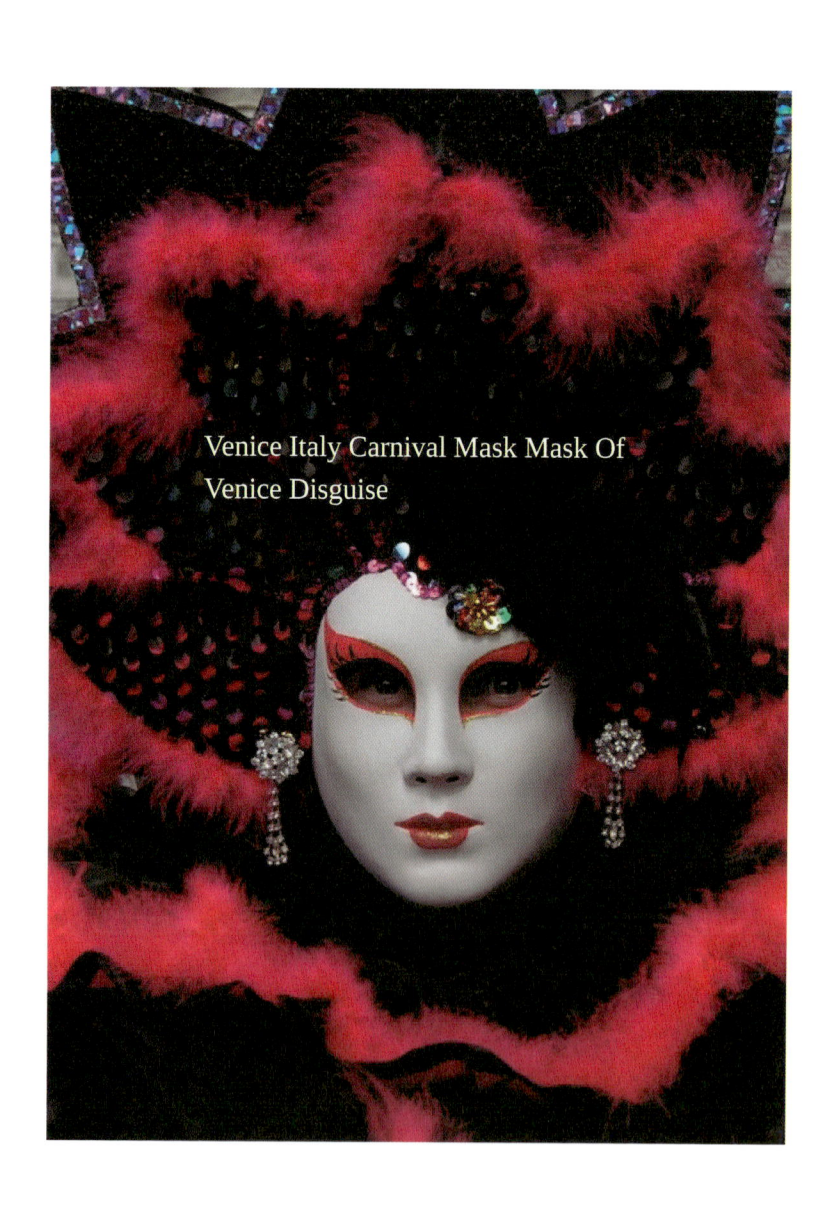

Venice Italy Carnival Mask Mask Of Venice Disguise

Mask Of Venice Carnival Italy

Venice Italy Car
Mask Mask Of V
Disguise

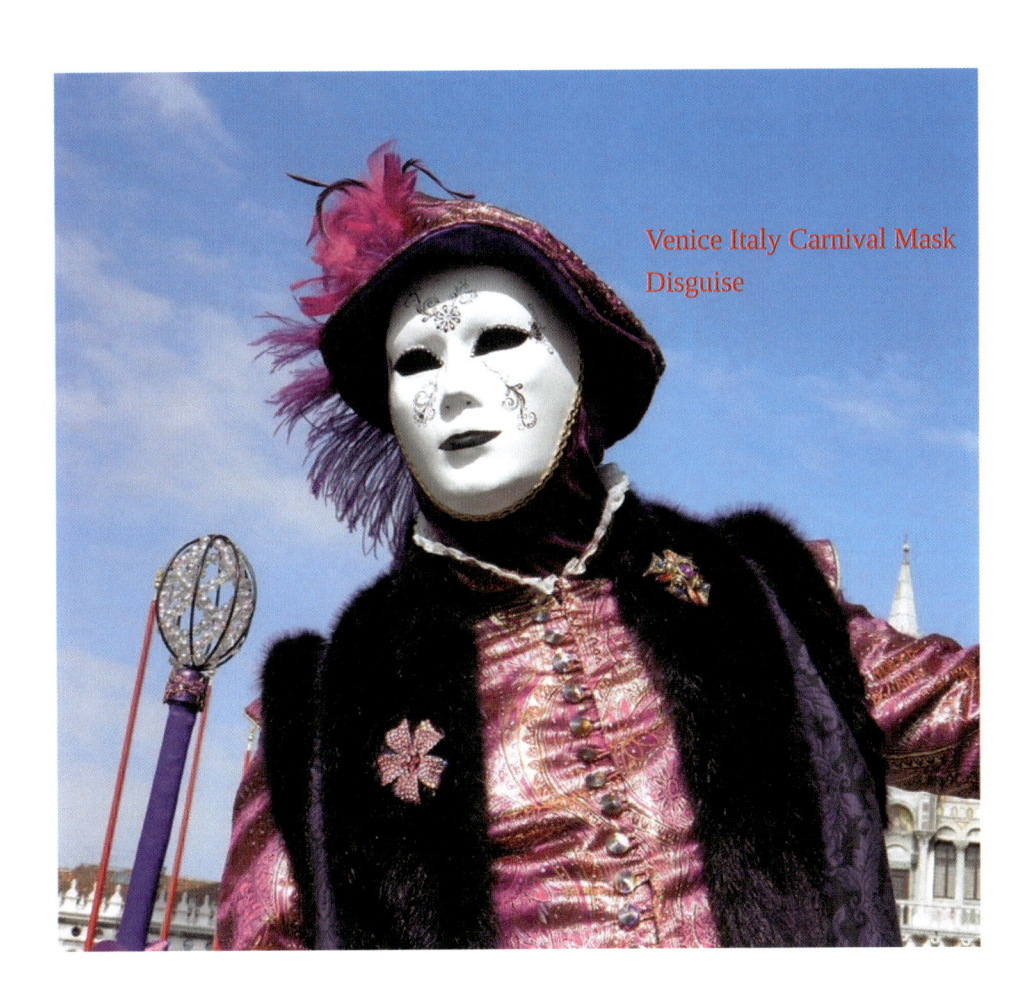

Venice Italy Carnival Mask Disguise

Italy Venice
Carnival

Venice Italy Carnival Mask Disguise

Venice Italy Carnival Mask Disguise

Venice Italy Carnival Mask Red Yellow Disguise

Carnival Venice Mask
Ug

Mask Of Venice
Masks Disguise

Venice Italy Carnival

Carnival Mask Disguise
Venice

Venice Mask Carnival Costumes

Carnival Venice Mask Reflection

Carnival Venice Masks Mask Of Venice Disguise

Carnival Venice
Hallia Venezia
Mask Costume

Venice Carnival Italy

Carnival Of Venice
Mask Of Venice Masks

Mask Red Lady Woman Human Carnival Masks Palace

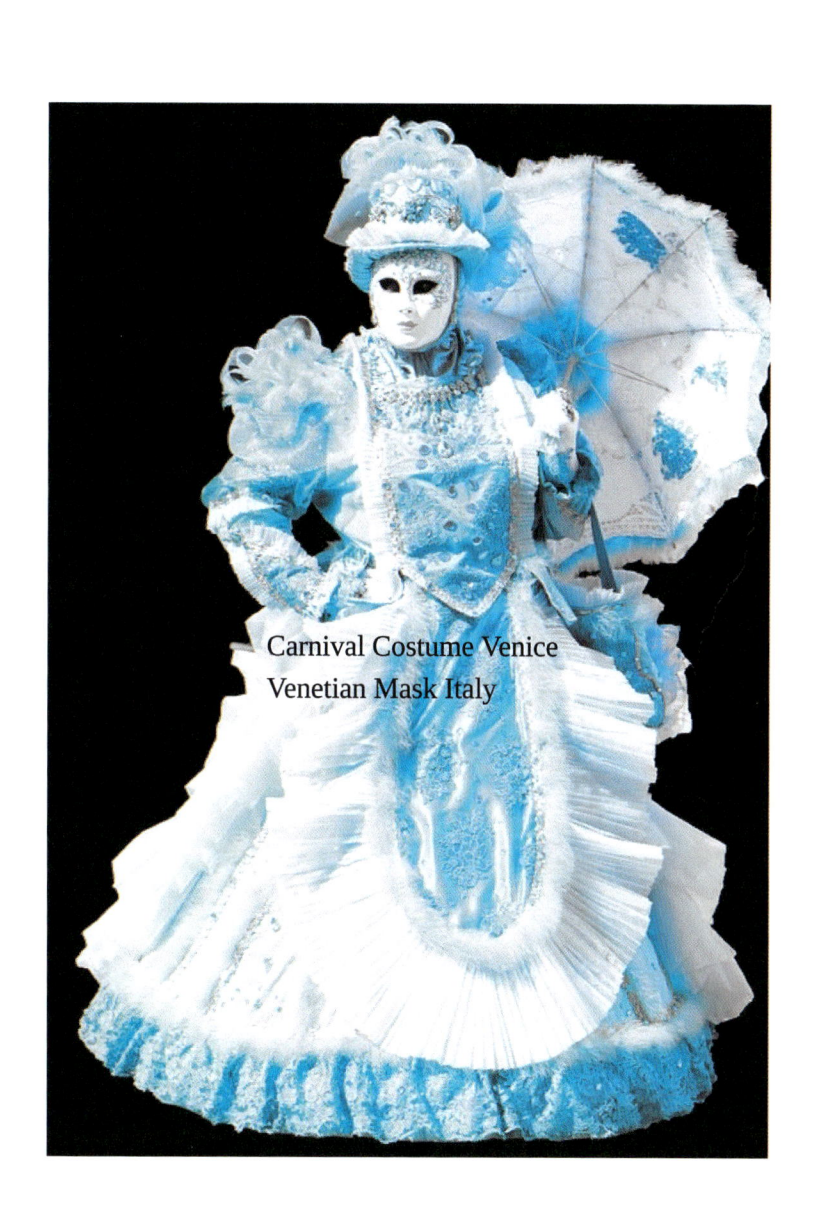

Carnival Costume Venice
Venetian Mask Italy

Carnival Venice Costume Mask Panel Gold

Venice Masks Carnival Italia

Venice Italy Carnival Mask
Disguise

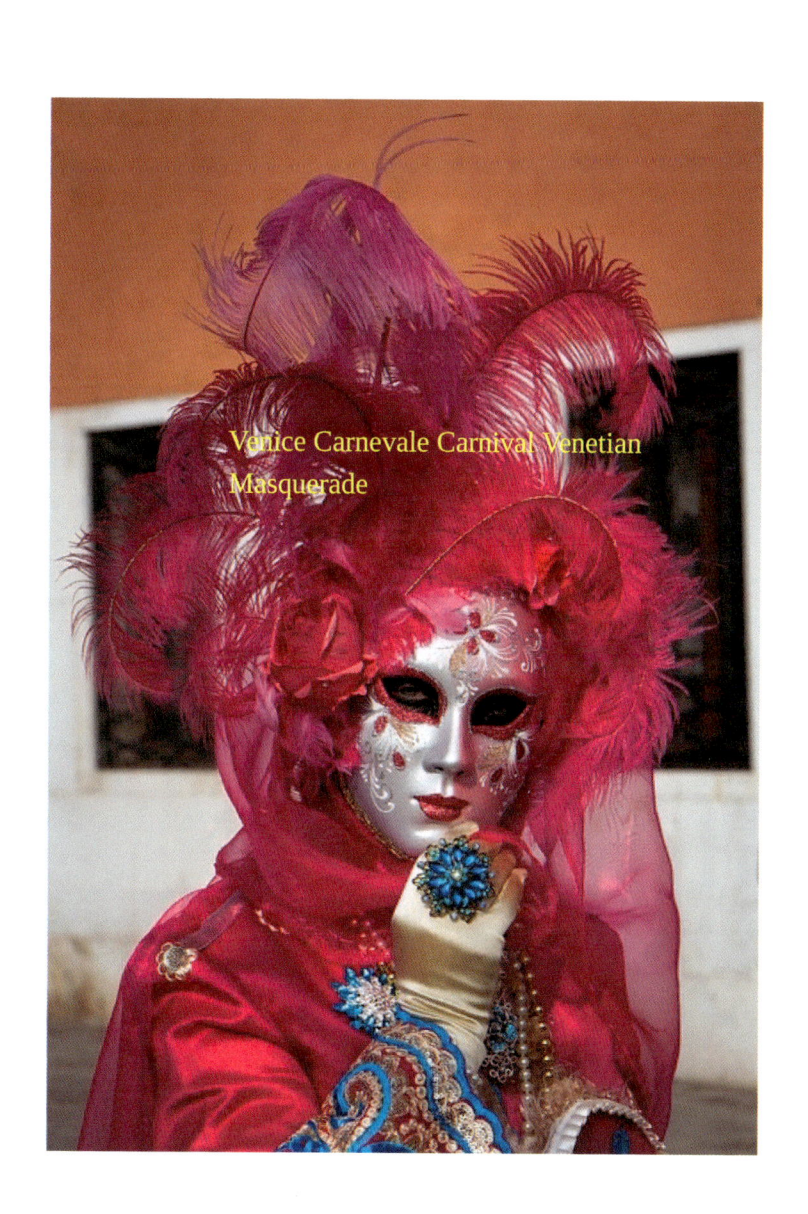

Venice Carnevale Carnival Venetian Masquerade

Italy Venice Carnival

Venice Italy Carnival Mask Disguise

Venice Carnevale
Carnival Venetian
Masquerade

Venice Italy Carniva
Mask Of Venice Dis

Carnival Venice Carnival
Venice Masks Italy

Carnival Mask Woman
Venice Italian Costume

Venice Mask
Carnival Italy
Venezia

Carnival Venice Mask Carnival Of Venice Italy

Masks Carnival Venice
Carnival Of Venice Italy

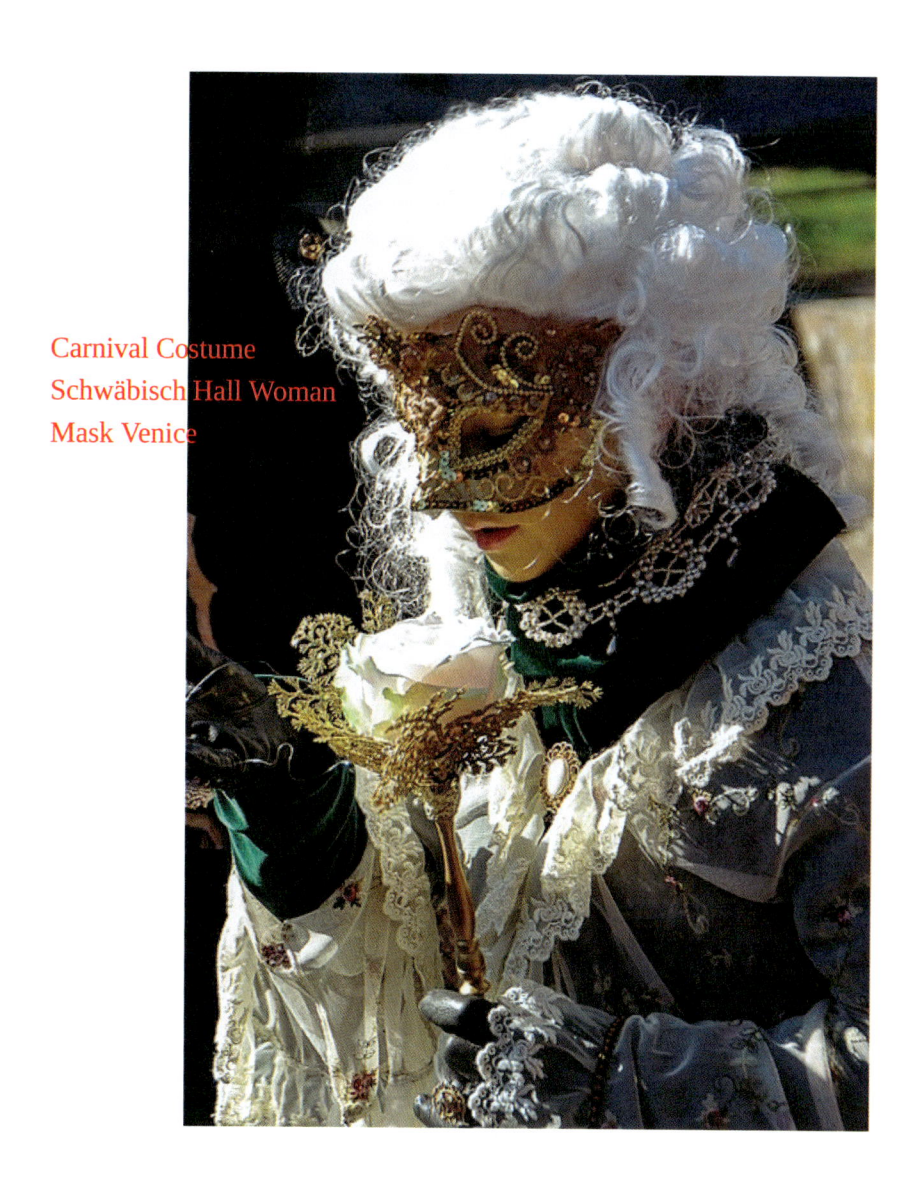

Carnival Costume
Schwäbisch Hall Woman
Mask Venice

Venice Italy
Carnival Mask
Colors Disguise

Carnival Masks Venice Carnival Of Venice Italy

Carnival Venice Dance Mask
Music Dancers Human

Masks Venice Carnival

Mask Carnival Venice Carnival Of Venice Italy

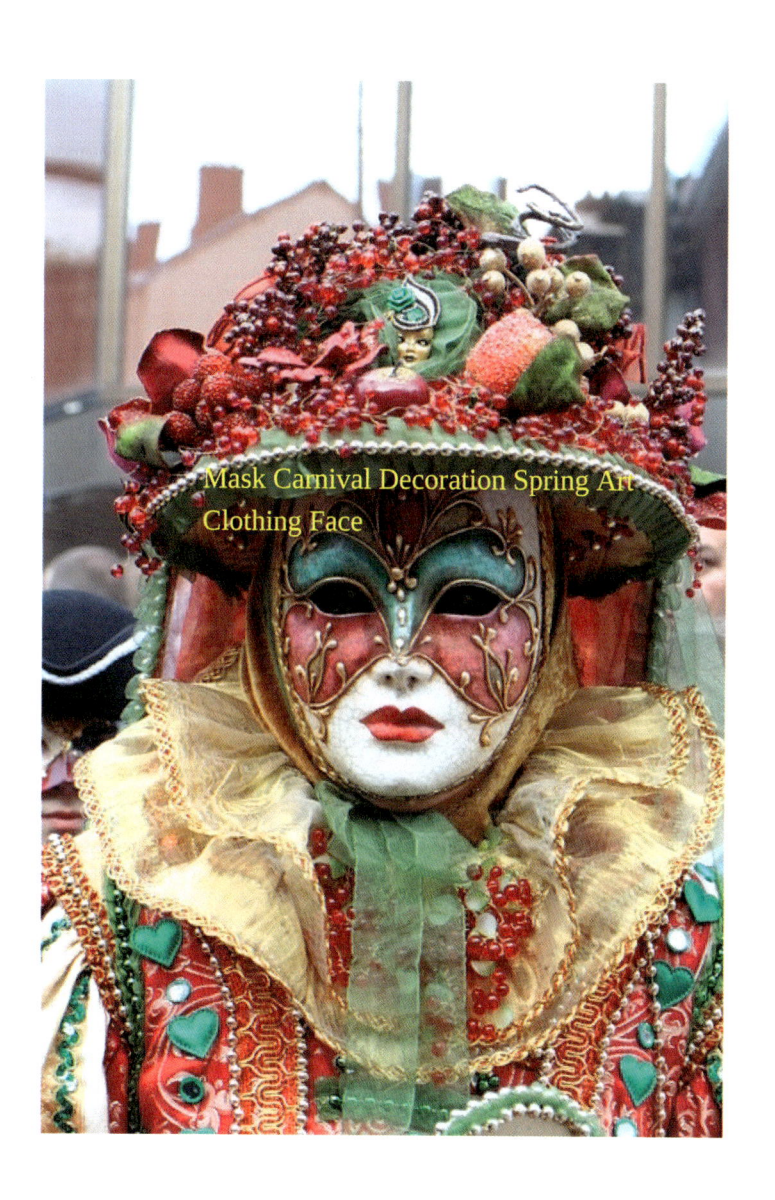

Mask Carnival Decoration Spring Art Clothing Face

Carnival Venice Mask

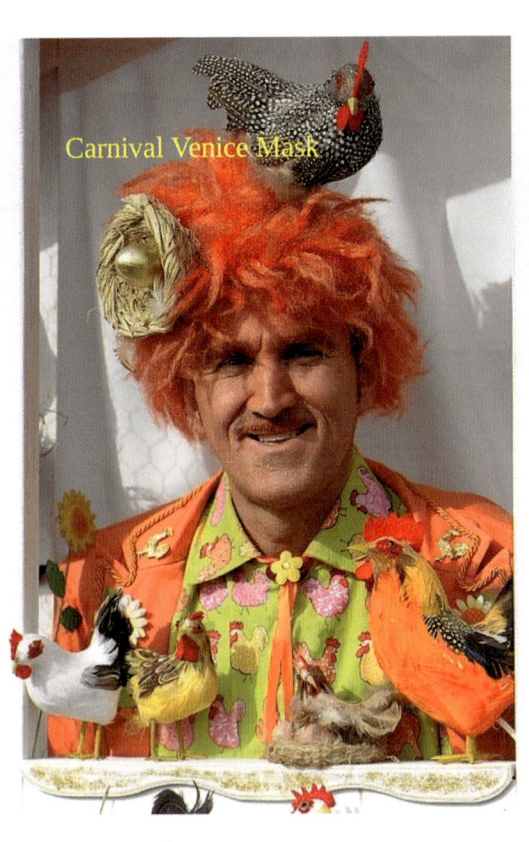

Mask Face Clothing Carnival Palace Decoration Art

Carnival Mask Figure
Ritual Venice Italy

Mask Decoration Face The Faces Of Harlequin People

Carnival
Mask
Disguise
Venice

Mask Carnival Face
Palace Art Cover
Festival

Masks Venice Carnival Venetian Mask

Venetian Mask Carnival Venice Face Decoration Fun

Carnival Costume
Schwäbisch Hall Whi[te]
Headdress

Mask Face Clothing Cover Carnival Masks Palace

Venice Carnival Mask Woman Italy Wig Spring

Carnival Venice Carnival Of Venice Mask Italy

Carnival Masks
Venice Carnival
Of Venice Italy

Venice Carnival Mask
Woman Italy Wig
Blonde

Mask Face Clothing Cover Carnival Palace Spring

Carnival Costume Pink Mask
Venice Schwäbisch Hall

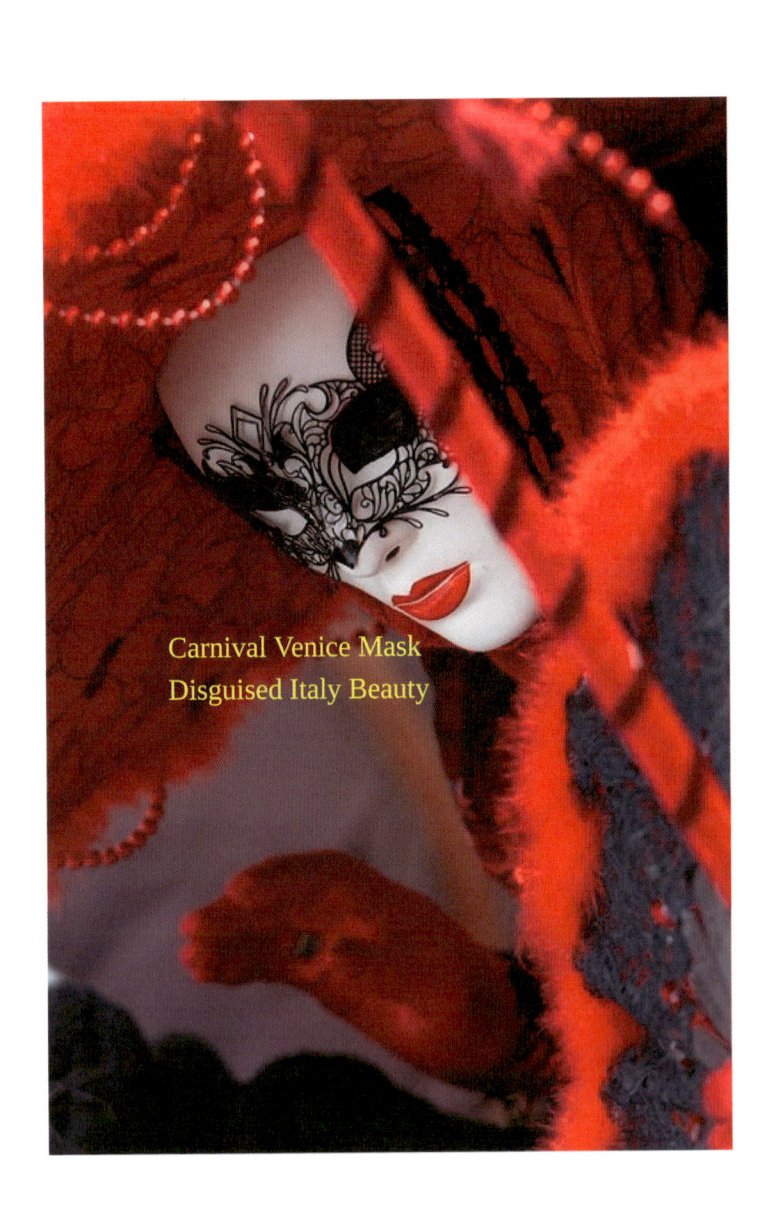

Carnival Venice Mask
Disguised Italy Beauty

Masks Venice Carnival Venetian Mask

Carnival Schwäbisch Hall Masks Women Colorful

Mask Carnival Venice Carnival Of Venice Italy

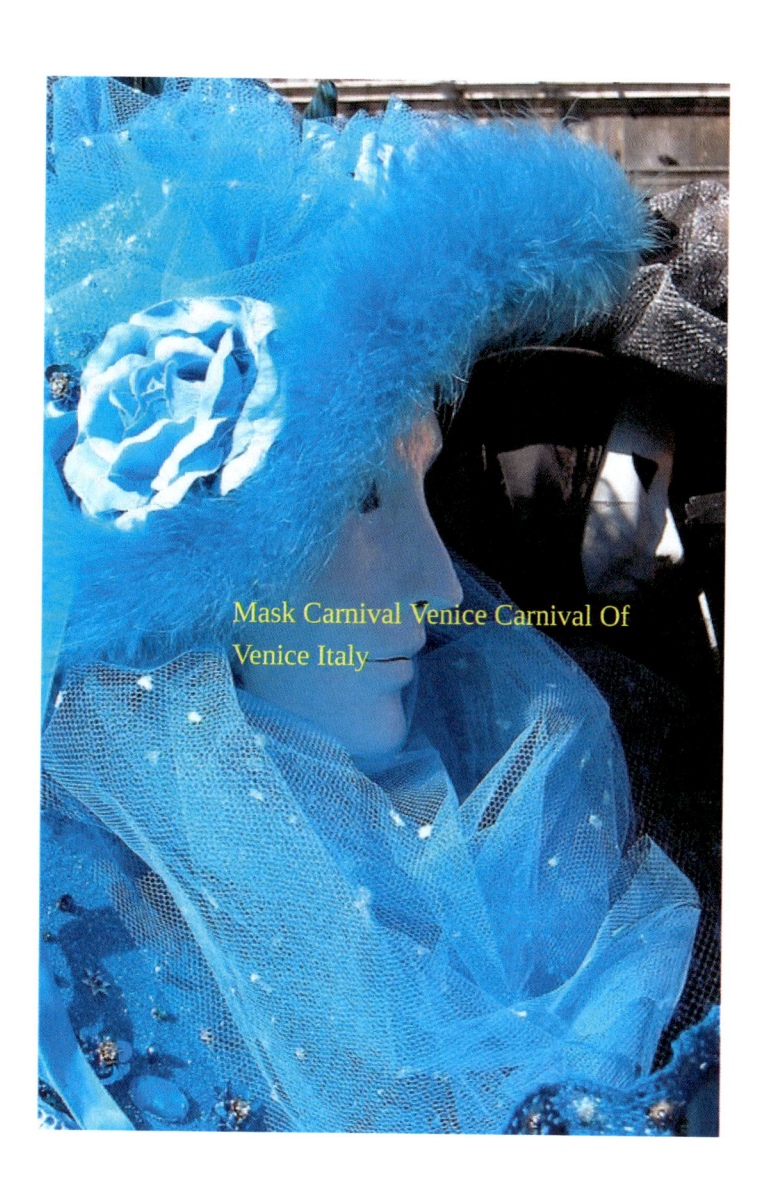

Venice Mask Carnival Colors Lovely Red Feather

Carnival Mask
Venice Rosa Rose
2015 Fun Confetti

Mask Carnival
Decoration Art Face
Spring Woman

Venice Masks Ca Carnival Masquerade Venetian Mask

Carnival Mask Venice Carnival Of Venice Italy

Venice Taly
Mask Blue
Face Carnival

Mask Carnival Venice

Photographer Carnival Venice

Carnival Mask Venice Rosa
Rose 2015 Fun Confetti

Carnival Venice
Carnival Of
Venice Masks
Italy

Carnival Venice
Mask Carnival Of
Venice Italy

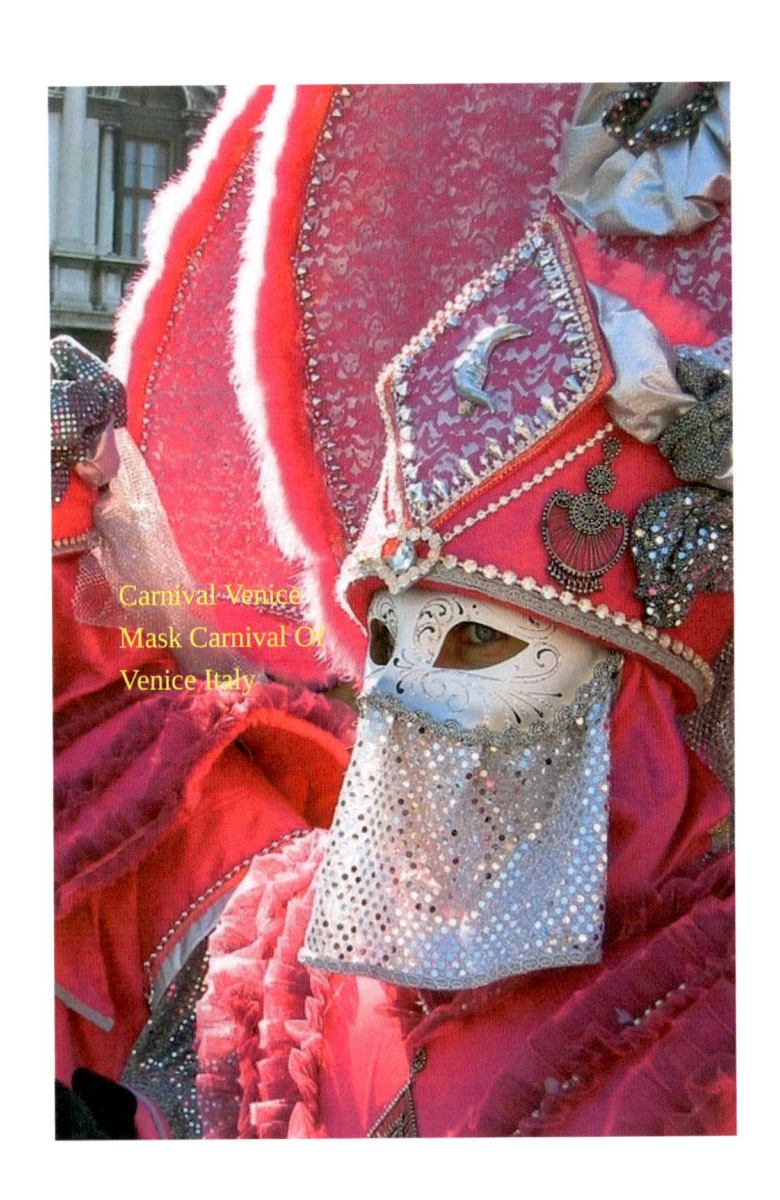

Mask Carnival Venice Mysterious Close Romance

Traditionally Costu
Carnival Panel Fool

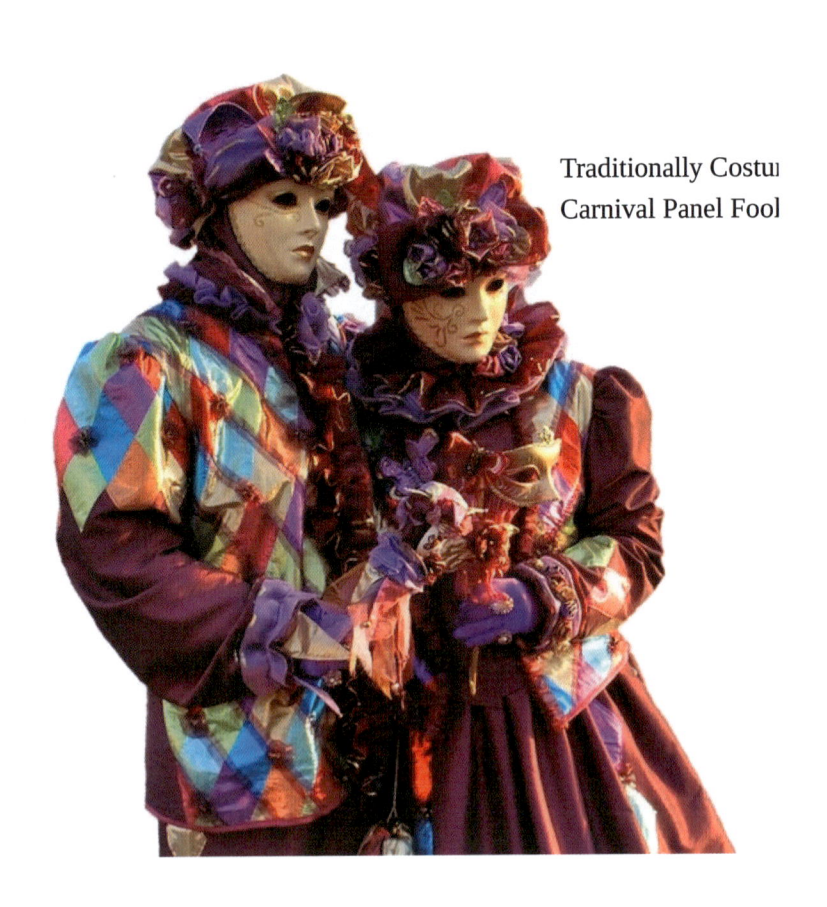

Background Isolated Pleasure Costume Traditionally

Human Waters Traditionally Costume Carnival Panel

Hide Costume Mystery
Masked Ball Carnival Venice

Mask Carnival Venice

Masks Carnival Of Venice Masks Of Venice

Mask Mask Of Venice Carnival Of Venice Venice

Mask Of Venice
Carnival Of Venice
Masks

Mask Venice
Carnival Italy
Venetian Mask
Face

Mask Carnival Venice

Masks Mask Of Venice Carnival Venice Carnival

Carnival Of Venice Mask
Of Venice Masks
Disguise

Mask Of Venice
Venice Masks Dis

Masks Carnival Of
Venice Mask Of Venice

Carnival Venice Costume Masquerade

Mask Venice Carnival Of Venice Mask Of Venice

Mask Of Venice Carnival Of Venice Masks Disguise

Carnival Of Venice
Mask Of Venice Masks

Masks Carnival Of Venice Masks Of Venice

Mask Venice Carnival Venetian Mask Costume Italy

Tags Separated By A
Venice Carnival Cos

Carnival Of Venice
Masks Mask Of
Venice Disguise

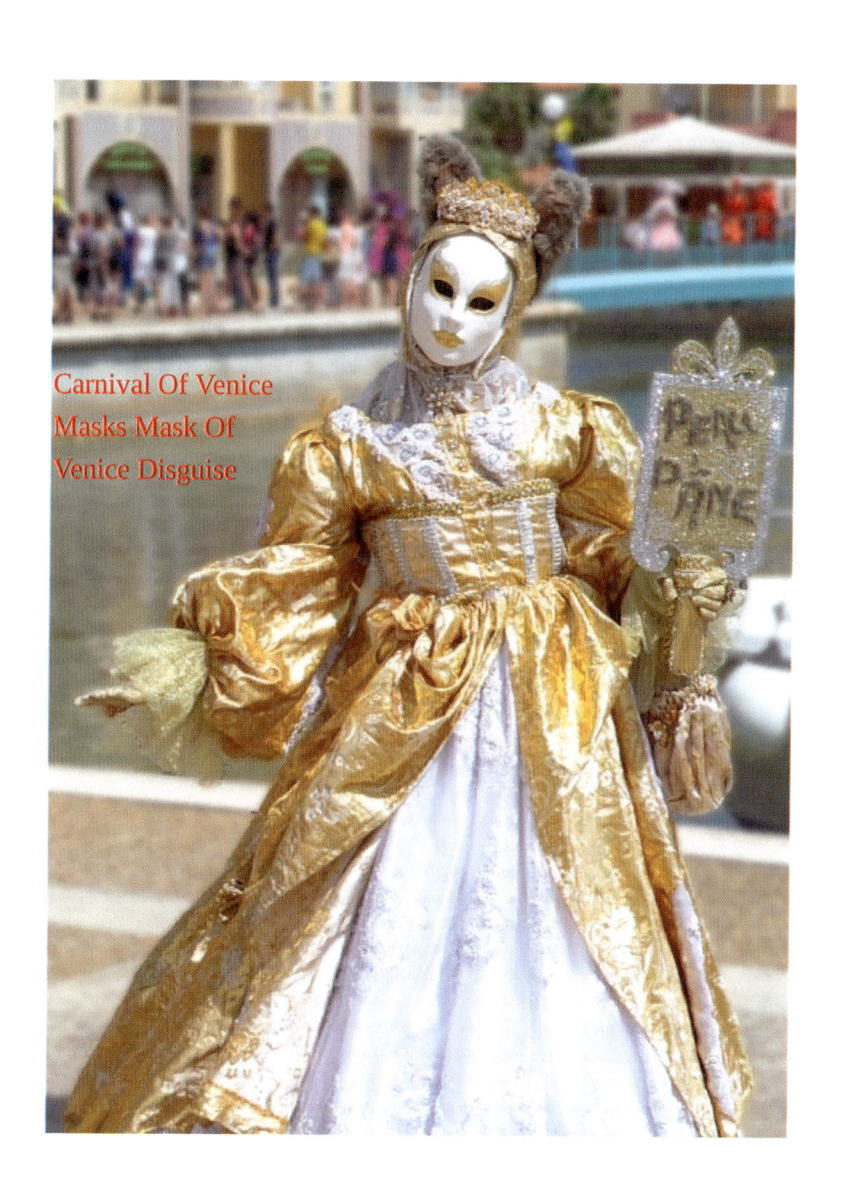

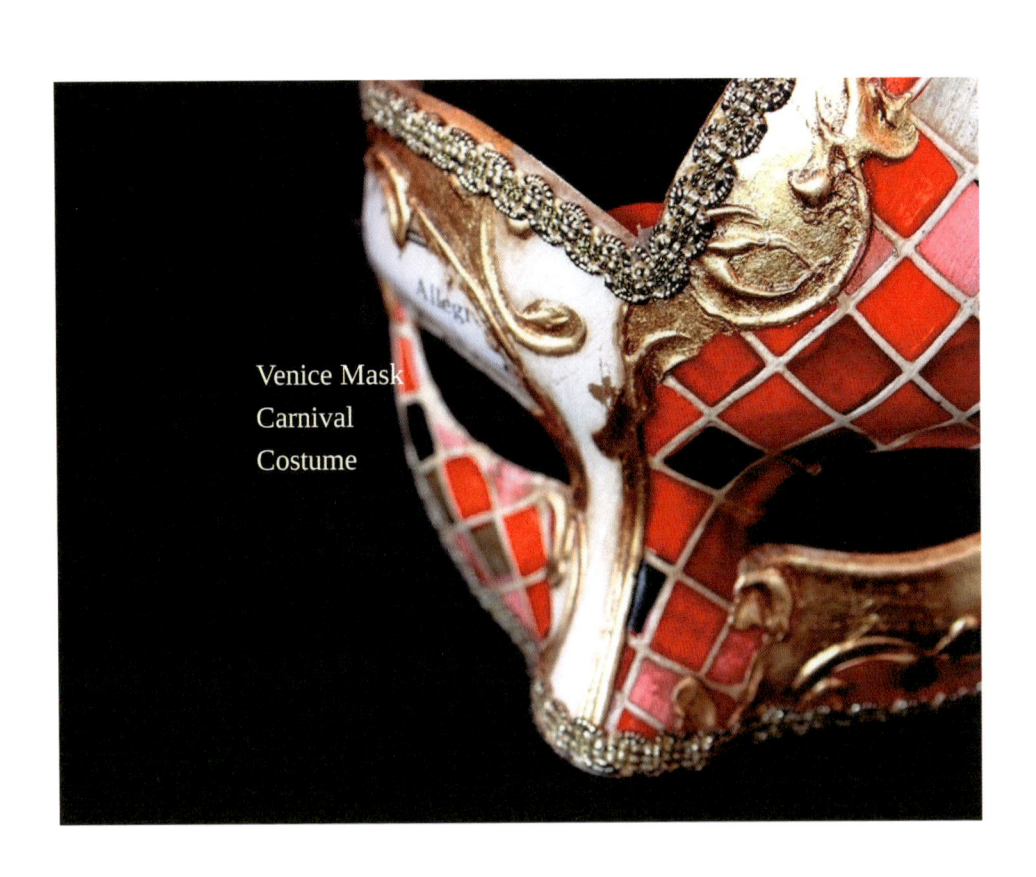

Venice Mask
Carnival
Costume

Venice Masks Tourism Italy Carnival

Carnival Of Venice Mask Of Venice Masks Disguise

Mask Disguise Carnival
Mask Of Venice Costume

Mask Carnival Venice Colors

Carnival Venice Venetian Disguise Mask Of Venice

Masks Mask Of Venice Carnival Venice

Carnival Masks Venetian Disguise Annecy

Venice Carnival Mask Part
Masquerade Festival

Mask Venice Carnival

Venice Carnival
Costume Mask Italy
Panel

Mask
Carnival
Venice

Carnival Venice Mask
Masks Disguise Costume

Masks
Carnival
Venice

Venice Italy Carnival Mask
Mask Of Venice Disguise

Venice Italy Carnival Mask Disguise

Venice Carnival Mask
Costume Disguise Masks Fun

Venice Masks
Carnival Italy
Costume
Venezia

Mask Carnival Venice

Hallia Venezia Costume
Carnival Schwäbisch Hall

Venice Carnival Mask
Men's Italy Costume
Hat

Venice Mask Venezia Carnival Costume Headdress

Printed in Great Britain
by Amazon